101 COMMUNIST JOKES

THE COMMUNIST MANIFESTO PART TWO

Tarl Warwick
2021

COPYRIGHT AND DISCLAIMER

100% Soy free!

FOREWORD

Communism is a funny ideology. Sure, the *results* of communism aren't funny- after all, Pol Pot slaughtered about a third of his own nations' population, Mao once caused a famine that killed ten million or more Chinese people because he decided people should exterminate sparrows, and then locusts came and ate their crops. Josef Stalin- who was a rapist and sexual degenerate- was responsible for roughly 20,000,000 deaths as he decided to randomly shuffle around ethnic groups in the USSR, to break their perceived ethnic homogeneity.

But that wasn't *real* communism, communists assure us.

Sometime, just for kicks, you should have a "conversation" with a communist- I use that term loosely; a lot of what you'll hear more closely resembles the babbling incoherence of a two year old toddler than it does an issuance from an adult human being- then bring up some of the funny things in this book. Or you can always read their own literature; the amount of psychobabble in them tends to be pretty high end, which shows the huge difference between leftist *leaders* and *followers*. The leaders rely on the followers being as dumb as rocks in order to foist their own perversions off on people.

Imagine, if you will, living in a world in which your perception of the things around you is nearly an inverse of any objective reality which could be defined. This is how the leftist muddles through their existence. The victims they call abusers, and they perceive abusers as victims. Often well off, they conceive of themselves as part of a workers' army. Often physically weak, the compare themselves to the red guard. Doomed to work to death in a collective farm or gulag if their worldview was ever adopted, they think instead that they would have a nice comfy little office with lots of vodka and some contraband imported luxury items as they enjoy life as a regional party head who doesn't have to live in a commie bloc Stalinka.

When I first set about making this little booklet I had initially planned to just write "communism" on each of 101 pages in different fonts. This would be the joke; then I realized that this was a low effort move and the sort of thing you'd normally expect from an intellectually lazy commie. But I'm a good capitalist, and I figured it would be more fun to actually crack a few wry one liners at the leftoids' expense. Initially solely to lampoon communists, I decided to just ridicule leftists in general, both because they deserve it and because there's no one universal definition of communism so, I guess I can just call *anyone* a commie if I want to.

It is worth noting in this obviously satirical work (I have to point that out, communists do not comprehend humor!) that communism these days has merged with globalism in general and it is no longer your grandpas' ethnic or nationalistic movement and now has tainted even supposedly capitalistic western nations. It is the responsibility of all people to condemn, revile, ridicule, and expose the menace wherever it is found. Let the ridicule begin! Here are 101 of the BEST communist jokes ever!

101 COMMUNIST JOKES

JOKE #1: Communism!

That's the joke! Communism is a joke!

JOKE #2: Karl Marx

He was a joke too. A pervert and armchair expert, he barely studied most of the subjects he thought of himself as being versed in, and spent years mooching off his slightly less intellectually bankrupt friend. No lover of mens' beard care products (or conditioner), Karl Marx is perhaps best known for spawning an ideology responsible for 100,000,000 deaths (give or take a few million)- something he would likely approve of. His theory was- funnily- derived from his ignorance of Anthropology- something which makes sense, since he never once physically interacted with the tribes he based his conception of "primitive communism" on. It is not clear whether his scraggly pirate beard came from being too friggin' lazy to shave it or if he was making some sort of demented fashion statement.

JOKE #3: Critical Race Theory

It isn't a theory, it isn't critical that anyone learn about it, and it's racist. Sort of defeats its stated purpose except for the being influenced by Marxism part.

JOKE #4: Leftist economics

If you want to manage an economy it helps to actually understand how economics work!

JOKE #5: Stalin

Imagine being such a twisted commie that even a lot of commies don't want to be associated with you and vehemently look for ways to prove to people that your ideology isn't even communism. He was good friends with Adolf Hitler until Hitler decided to invade Poland, then he mooched off the US while marching millions of peasants to their death, getting killed by the nazis at about a 4 to 1 ratio. He is considered a strategic genius by tankies.

JOKE #6: "Real Communism"

Every possible iteration and variant of communism has been tried but each one is opposed by all other communist groups on the basis that it isn't actually communism. Since communism is supposed to be the innate and natural state of mankind this is one hell of an admission of failure.

JOKE #7: Engels

For a supposedly slightly more intelligent counterpart to Karl Marx, Engels sure didn't seem to have an issue with Marx grifting off of his income.

JOKE #8: Trotsky

Imagine being a commie, knowing commies are violent and territorial, and that you have a massive target on your back, but you still get icepick'd. What a loser.

JOKE #9: CIA Subversion

Every time that a communist (or generally leftist) system collapses, the spooks at the CIA are inevitably blamed. While the CIA coke snorters are undoubtedly involved in overthrowing various regimes, the communist does not believe that any other method exists for their glorious system to fail. Communism is so weak that a few well funded cocaine addicts have repeatedly thwarted them at all turns. The CIA is like Inspector Gadget inexplicably stopping Doctor Claw episode after episode no matter what technological devices are deployed against him, all while constantly cracking dad jokes and waving a robotic umbrella around.

JOKE #10: Soviet poverty claims

The USSR uplifted many people out of poverty by killing the most poor and weak of them. This is considered funny, by leftists.

JOKE #11: Pol Pot

Pol Pot is hardly funny but the madness with which he operated is amusing in a sort of grave humor way. Pol Pot was so insane that the Vietnamese communists invaded him. Ironically, he was initially backed as the legit leader of Cambodia by the US government, showing that McCarthy was right and that the worst hard line commies had, by that time, already begun influencing the "land of the free." Pol Pot was a lover of landscaping and frequently decorated his properties with piles of human skulls. I wish this was a hyperbolic reference.

JOKE #12: Mao

Chairman Mao was a fat imbecile who decided that the entire nation should melt down every metal implement available for industrial needs. This resulted in a hoard of pig iron so worthless that it was unusable for any practical purpose. He also lost a war against sparrows and locusts, and killed thirty million or so Chinese citizens just through starvation and pestilence. He didn't have an issue with this because as with many communists he saw the value of human lives other than his own as being non-existent.

JOKE #13: Xi Jinping

This commie is only slightly more fat than Chairman Mao and half as intelligent, essentially proving communism evolves in reverse. He is very sensitive about his looks and has had people killed for comparing him to Winnie the Pooh even though the resemblance is uncanny. Those same initially Chinese-sourced cartoons portrayed Barack Obama as Tigger, which was "totally not" a thinly guised racial epithet.

JOKE #14: Tito

Some communists believe communism can work because Titoism actually kind of did; they pair this with ignoring his co-sponsoring of the non aligned movement, his continuously mounting tensions with Stalin (who he threatened to assassinate) and his technical Yugo-nationalistic sentiments. Other communists, mad that he succeeded because he abandoned communist economics, consider him a fascist. He did more to stop communism than most Western powers did. Bravo Tito!

JOKE #15: Chernobyl Power Plant

A massive and astonishing feat of Soviet engineering that was very likely deliberately sabotaged in order to cover up the failures of over-the-horizon radar. Ironically the power plant is more useful now to the Ukrainians than it ever was to the Soviets since it generates a lot of capitalistic tourist income.

JOKE #16: The Chinese Military

If copying others' homework was a skill the Chinese military is the master. Plus their aircraft carrier still uses a ramp. If you mention this to the more militaristic communists they will immediately go insane and start talking about how the US military celebrates pride month.

JOKE #17: Anarcho-communism

Communism doesn't actually fight to abolish the state since every commie believes they will be the leader of some committee after the revolution, and they are all secret tankies. Nonetheless, communists use the term "anarchism" to appeal to edgy college kids and druggies.

JOKE #18: Antifa

Fighting fascism is easy. First, you have to gang up on an elderly lady and beat her down, then you have to flip off some cops and poop on the ground and smear it on yourself. This is actually more sane than many other communist sub-ideologies.

JOKE #19: BLM

BLM was influenced heavily by Marxism. This was self admitted by several of its founders. Now its current leaders mainly seem to exist to extort cash from corporations, which pay them to get good press coverage.

JOKE #20: The Soviet Union

The closest communism has come to maintaining any semblance of long-lasting influence, the Soviet Union began with several genocides and continued with a few more. Those lucky enough not to be massacred were then strapped with a half century of poverty and intellectual suppression.

JOKE #21: Ivory Tower Professors

There are a lot of "academics" who only have jobs because executive-minded college deans feel sorry for them. Most of them are communists or socialists and consider the piece of paper they spent 50,000 dollars to get as an "achievement" in life.

JOKE #22: Cuba

An intermediate-sized island that could develop a tourist industry alone capable of sustaining growth, Cuba was overrun by communists, was the flashpoint that almost destroyed civilization, and is still run by tinhorn autocrats to this day. Their poverty is blamed by leftists on an embargo that only affects US trade and then only on luxury items.

JOKE #23: Fidel Castro

Once a military man, this fossilized and decreasingly coherent vegetable eventually keeled over and the pickup truck toting his casket broke down on the way. A perfect metaphor for communism.

JOKE #24: Che Guevara

A lightning rod for the admiration of college kids who did not study history, Che Guevara was an asthmatic coward who ended up getting killed and his mangled corpse was strapped to a CIA helicopter for shipping. He was fond of executing civilians, which makes him a fairly straight-forward commie.

JOKE #25: The Rosenbergs

Julius and Ethel stole atomic plans from the USA to hand over to the Soviets, presumably because they realized the Soviets were too stupid to develop atomic weapons on their own, thus beginning the era of mutually assured destruction. Thanks to these individuals (who are rarely mentioned in history textbooks), trillions were wasted and entire islands bombed til they practically glowed in the dark.

JOKE #26: Gorbachev

A man reviled by communists while ironically having saved Soviet citizens from some of the worse aspects of Soviet ideology. Now they have food, more or less.

JOKE #27: The US Democratic Party

Sure, most Democrats aren't communists, but what can we do other than guffaw at a political party that thinks tolerating commies and socialists in its ranks while swearing up and down it isn't socialism is a viable political concept? These sleazy empty suits have spent years using left wing college kids as cheap pawns and now are getting their comeuppance.

JOKE #28: "Progressives"

Nothing says progress like adopting "just some" of the failed fiscal and social policies which have previously destroyed a dozen nations.

JOKE #29: Tankies

Utter morons who lionize the Soviet Army, even though its entire winning streak was solely the result of capitalistic US Lend-Lease programs requiring massive private infrastructure and Uncle Sam's deep pockets. Were it not for that, the USSR would have been fighting the Luftwaffe with biplanes. In fact, at first, it did! Pew pew!

JOKE #30: Starbucks Marxists

Also known as "Champagne socialists." Effete trust fund suburban kids who have never worked a day in their lives who only endorse leftist economics because they were told it would help the poor that they never met, and the oppressed they never really want to associate with.

JOKE #31: Breadtube

Also known as breadliners. A collective of astroturfed, normally well off vloggers who seek to "deradicalize" people by converting them to Marxism. Not one of them would survive communism though, as their body mass index is usually far too excessive. They see no irony in begging for donations from their gullible fans, or using platforms run by cut-throat and supposedly capitalistic corporations.

JOKE #32: The NBA

Basketball is big in China and this forces the NBA to suck them off at all times. Some players seem to have an awful lot of respect for China despite its routine human rights abuses and use of slavery- probably because they get big bucks from companies exploiting that slavery and child labor.

JOKE #33: Tienanmen Square

I just inserted this joke in this book so it'd be illegal for anyone in China to have a copy, including their censorship-pushing army of CCP shills. Enjoy the gulag, my redistributionist friend! Free Tibet!

JOKE #34: Helicopters

The mortal enemy of communists.

JOKE #35: Bernie Sanders

A washed up and incoherent coot who has ranted about the same three or so issues since the 1970s but still believes the great peoples' revolution is coming. He spent his honeymoon in the USSR, and everyone wishes he had remained there. He rants about the importance of socialist medical care while openly endorsing massively sugary and nutrition free ice cream to anyone near him. Everyone expects he will be the one that serves Joe Biden the scoop that finally bursts his next aneurysm.

JOKE #36: The Berlin Wall

The ultimate self-satirizing move the Soviets ever made, giving limitless opportunities for Western nations to decry communism. One of the few examples in history where a supposedly prosperous and growing power attempts to build a wall system to keep people from leaving. One family escaped by using a hot air balloon that did not even have basic controls, proving that mid 18th century technology is better than communism.

JOKE #37: Alexandria Ocasio-Cortez

A brainless girl who imagines herself to be a considerable political force but at the end of the day is constantly muzzled by the neoliberals who actually control the US Democratic Party. The less intelligent, far less attractive version of Jane Fonda.

JOKE #38: Bù wàng chūxīn

A Chinese term roughly meaning "stay true to the mission." As with virtually every other "patriotic" term in mankinds' history it is an empty slogan. Similar to "build back better", "patriot act", "clean coal", or "I did not inhale."

JOKE #39: The Young Turks

A Youtube show run by Cenk Uygur, who was trolled massively during the 2018 midterms, when thousands of people showed up on the election live stream to post spoon emojis in the live chat, laughing about the US Democrats failing to retake the senate while losing more than half of their House majority.

JOKE #40: Joe Biden

A life-long tough-on-crime neoliberal who every US leftist held their nose to vote for. Then he had brutal diarrhea all over them and the US constitution and the economy, and most of them now hate him. Nonetheless because leftists have limited intellectual capabilities, most of them would probably vote for him again if CNN told them to do so.

JOKE #41: The corporate media

A series of supposedly private companies that openly collude with various governments and which pretend to be "progressive" to cater to the youth demographic, when they are all owned by billionaires and will push for war any time Uncle Sam or whoever else pays them cracks the whip.

JOKE #42: Wokeness

The level of ones' wokeness is synonymous with the level of ones' susceptibility to corporate and political propaganda. Corporations pretend to be "woke" in order to fool leftists into buying more materialistic junk.

JOKE #43: Socialism

1.) Communism rebranded to fool people.
2.) A half step to communism.
3.) Communism for trust funders.

JOKE #44: Cringe Fringe

A term for leftists which attention seek by constantly attempting to create definitions of what is "problematic", applying it to others and pretending to be offended. Those few who are genuinely offended and not pretending are prone to end up in insane asylums from time to time.

JOKE #45: China's Existence

It's actually West Taiwan.

JOKE #46: Workers

People who are assured they won't be sent to a gulag or a rock quarry when communists take control. Sadly they will be sent to a gulag or rock quarry.

JOKE #47: Equity

A buzzterm used by leftists that they insist is about elevating the lower classes but really is about dragging down those who have succeeded, as a form of ersatz-progress.

JOKE #48: State Capitalism

A buzzterm used by communists to deflect blame for when their system fails. Any system which fails (inevitably, under communism or socialism) is rebranded because it inevitably does not conform to the ever changing, malleable concept of "real" communism.

JOKE 49: The Bourgeois

Anyone who has more than one potato is considered bourgeois under a communist system. These enemies of revolution have somehow hoarded two or more potatoes and should be punished for anti-revolutionary activities.

JOKE #50: Dekulakization

The Soviets forced millions of people off their land and abused them because the Soviets did not understand how economics work. This is why tens of millions of people starved in the Soviet Union. People who would wither without their daily Starbucks n' Soy continue to idolize this move to this day, thinking people managing to "make it" under the Tsars were somehow subversive for doing so.

JOKE #51: Late Stage Capitalism

A common lemming-like chant which comes from leftists when nations and economic systems they have poisoned inevitably begin showing signs of stress and/or failure.

JOKE #52: Propaganda

This term is used to define any criticism of a left wing government or economic system. The irony is that this is, itself, actually propaganda.

JOKE #53: 1984

A book no communist has ever read. If they did they would interpret it as a user manual.

JOKE #54: "Anti-SJW" leftists

Grifters who no longer generally criticize censorship and who prefer to pal around with wealthy self-professed Marxists despite "totally just being social democrats."

JOKE #55: Alcoholism

Communist nations are usually overrun with alcoholism as peasants seek in vain to forget about their miserable lives. A few nations practicing communism have strict alcohol regulations to prevent this, but the citizens just turn to other drugs instead, or to masochistic depravity.

JOKE #56: Primitive Communism

The central basis for Marxist theory is that communism in the stateless form is innate and biologically normal- which defies every observable tendency of evolutionary theory. Marx lived and died too soon to see the unearthing of Catalhoyuk and Gobekli Tepe, which proved that mankind already was capable of mass organization many thousands of years prior to the rise of empires. At Catalhoyuk, primitive nationalism, family-centric tribalism, theocracy, and even possibly capitalism are all reflected, potentially in the remains... Literally every system other than the one Marx predicted would be followed that far back in the human timeline. Indeed, people 15,000 years ago were able to organize societies which remained stable, on a level no communist has ever yet achieved. In reality, communism remains primitive to this day.

JOKE #57: Western Imperialism

The notion that China, the USSR, and similar states, have never, ever invaded or subverted other nations, and that only the big bad United States and its lackeys have ever done so.

JOKE #58: Primitivism

A bizarre form of anarchism which roughly resembles a dumbed-down conception of the basic premise Pol Pot endorsed, in which people are meant to abandon modernity and return to the hominid stage of evolution. A stark denial of the long term basic idea of evolution, in favor of playing around with rocks and sticks. I suppose the rocks and sticks would be communally owned.

JOKE #59: Hippies

Sometimes wrongfully labeled communists by both right wingers who hate them and leftists seeking to befuddle college kids with marijuana and bright colors, few hippies ever promoted communism, and a lot of them ended up settling in the Pacific Northwest and becoming survivalistic anarcho-capitalists who bitterly hated the state and all forms of regulation.

JOKE #60: The Vietnam War

One giant SNAFU in which the US government fought communism by becoming more like communists, wasting years of time and tens of thousands of lives for absolutely nothing.

JOKE #61: James Bond

A brand that used to mainly be about stopping commies or evil scientists, and ridiculing them both, but will absolutely be going woke soon and will become unwatchable, corrupted, and stupid, just like Disneys "Star Wars" franchise, which deviates from enormous piles of potential canon in order to rehash the same trilogy over and over.

JOKE #62: Apple Inc.

A company which benefits from forced labor in China, where their factories at least in the past actually had nets outside the windows to prevent workers from committing suicide by jumping out. Chinese minerals mined in even-more-depraved North Korea are used in many of their products.

JOKE #63: Nike

A dumb and overpriced shoe brand. Sort of like the clothing equivalent of Apple but twice as obviously bought off.

JOKE #64: Big Tech

A conglomerate of tech firms based in California which once stood for free expression but now sound more and more like Beijing mouthpieces, pushing a social credit score system.

JOKE #65: California

A state in the United States slowly becoming more and more socialistic. As it does, more and more people leave. Politicians there are confused as to why that is happening. Sadly some Californians take their ideology with them, and they are beginning to infect other states with their madness.

JOKE #66: Colin Kaepernick

Famous for kneeling a few times. Also can run around and hold a ball at the same time. Very talented, for a leftist.

JOKE #67: Racist

A term used by leftist figures to describe anyone who dislikes them or their economic proposals. Also used by the US Democratic Party to describe anyone voting against their bills.

JOKE #68: CNN

The Commie News Network. A mouthpiece for globalism and tyranny, which lies to its viewers on a constant basis.

JOKE #69: Groucho Marx

Not actually a relative of Karl Marx, which should be obvious since he had a job and a sense of humor.

JOKE #70: The Weather Underground

A leftist terrorist group that bombed government buildings during the Vietnam War era, failing to accomplish anything. Totally-not-socialist politicians have sometimes been strangely close to some of its figures.

JOKE #71: Barack Obama

Totally not one of those eye-rollingly cringe college kids who toyed with communism and socialism before they realized how great being rich was.

JOKE #72: Nazis

Socialists. Socialists as always claim they weren't "really socialists." This is despite the NSDAP adopting explicitly redistributionist, centralized policies. Socialist FDR shared their love for race-based concentration camps.

JOKE #73: Social Democrats

Socialists too dishonest or afraid to use that term to describe themselves.

JOKE #74: Democratic Socialism

Socialism in which people vote socialists into power before they are lined up against a wall and shot, or sent to work in a gulag, as opposed to "normal" socialism where the socialists line them up or gulag them without needing to be voted into power, due to their numbers.

JOKE #75: The Nordic Model

Supposedly a form of socialism and held up by socialists as evidence their system can work. The Nordic Model is based partly on hyper-deregulation of the sort leftists in most of the world label fascistic.

JOKE #76: The Red Scare

A period in which the few people willing to address the elephant-in-the-room issue of socialist and communist influence over celebrities, military leaders, corporate heads, bankers, and politicians, were castigated as alarmists and as paranoid. While some of their claims were hyperbolic and discredited, they were later proven to have been at partially correct. Oops.

JOKE #77: Juche

The military-first communist offshoot system employed in North Korea. This results in a hyper-insularity in which trade and travel anywhere but with China is virtually nonexistent. Everyone has to serve in the military, which is good since nobody would sign up voluntarily to go on forced marches while receiving no more food than anyone else in the starving nation.

JOKE #78: COVID19

A virus which originated in China. Leftists in the United States got confused and thought that meant Donald Trump was responsible for its existence. Once said to come from people eating bats or pangolins, the same political and medical figures which vehemently denied it could have come from a Chinese virology lab have now reluctantly stated the obvious, that the initial outbreak being a few miles from said lab was "maybe not a coincidence."

JOKE #79: Punk Rock

Once listenable, this musical genre has devolved into whining and wokeness. No Green Day fan has ever apparently heard of GG Allin or Johnny Rotten.

JOKE #80: Food

Something rare in communist nations due to poor central planning, embezzlement, and inefficiency of distribution.

JOKE #81: Breadlines

Something Bernie Sanders praises and which were common in the Soviet Union. Under capitalism sometimes you have breadlines, but under socialism sometimes you have bread.

JOKE #82: Memes

The left self-satirizes constantly and leftist memes tend to follow one of two basic trajectories:

Memes so convoluted and over the top that a person will get bored even witnessing the meme. Often this takes the form of excessive text usage.

Memes which make a point so stupid and exploitable that it accidentally provides fodder for other people to make fun of it and/or the creator of the meme. (See "CHUD".)

It has been said that the left can't meme. This is undeniably the case.

JOKE #83: Purity Spiraling

This term describes when a group continues to become more and more extreme or incoherent over time as the more fanatical members compete for limited attention, resources, etc. This is currently happening to the US Democratic Party, causing them to plummet in popularity- which is no more than they deserve.

JOKE #84: The Lincoln Project

An assortment of laughable rich dudes who once pretended to be disaffected Republicans, and whose fans imagine them to have a sort of outsized impact in the US political system. Their takes are about as you'd expect from out of touch, wealthy, pudgy middle aged white guys- cringe wall to wall.

JOKE #85: Soy

Soy is a perpetual left-adjacent term because so many leftists seem to enjoy veganism and fad dieting. Most Marxists do not share this tendency, indeed some of them seem to go out of their way to eat unhealthy food just to differentiate themselves from the "weakling" soy left. This is why so many Marxist commentators are fat, greasy slobs.

JOKE #86: Fact Checking

Engaging in propaganda and lying in order to deceive people, often conducted by the legacy media.

JOKE #87: Andrew Cuomo

An alleged rapist and confirmed killer of grandmas, he currently serves as the governor of New York, and somehow has escaped repercussions for lying to his whole state. That is likely because his entire state is used to being lied to and does not see this as a problem. That, in turn, is probably why New York continues to vote heavily for the US Democratic Party.

JOKE #88: Michael Avenatti

Once held up on a pedestal by the entire lamestream media and the US Democratic Party, Avenatti was eventually sued by a high profile former client and then got put in prison for extortion. Since then there has been a virtual media blackout about him because it isn't good to have praised an extortionist and toyed with the idea that they should run for the presidency. Basta!

JOKE #89: Inflation

Something which everyone used to understand was generally not good except in small amounts, but is now foretold to be "just fine" or even "good" to have in excessive amounts by propagandists now that the US government is run by a liberal with no economic comprehension.

JOKE #90: ACAB

An acronym chant beloved by leftists until their home gets broken into and- gun hating as they tend to be- they have to cower in a closet and wait for the sheriff to show up and save them.

JOKE #91: Workers' Rights

Something cherished by leftists until it comes to those workers not wanting to unionize or if the worker suddenly starts their own business.

JOKE #92: Utopia

Something communists especially seek to achieve. They think this will best be accomplished by slaughtering much of the population and ripping apart the concept of the constitutional system.

JOKE #93: Diversity

A buzz term used by corporations to sell things to leftists, and used by governments to silence dissent. An abstract concept in which it is believed that a nation or business cannot function unless it looks like a bowl of Skittles.

JOKE #94: Milk, Cauliflower, The OK Sign, and Cartoon Frogs

Just a few of the things which have recently been labeled racist or bigoted by leftists who were tricked into that belief by internet trolls who scorn and ridicule them.

JOKE #95: The Bush Family

Supposedly a bunch of gun loving redneck cowboys, but actually a massively wealthy blue-blooded Connecticut lineage peopled by life-long mafioso crooks who are just really good at acting. Except Jeb Bush; he seems to genuinely be a dumb rube.

JOKE #96: "Resist"

A catch-phrase wielded by leftists on the internet, who believe that they are part of the rebel alliance, or Dumbledore's Army, even though they're really just doing the bidding of billionaires and war-happy politicians who are exploiting them while making them feel good about being exploited. The only thing they're really resisting is basic common sense.

JOKE #97: Jingoism

When anyone not in a communist or socialist nation is pro-military or supports a generally beefy national defense. Juche meanwhile is fine though.

JOKE #98: Who Will Build the Roads?

A rhetorical and joking statement usually used in a mocking manner by libertarians and conservatives, to indicate disdain at leftists who claim that without ever larger government, society will collapse into disarray. However, sometimes, leftists use similar (and very poor) arguments to back up their claim that the government needs to be expanded to prevent some problem or another actually caused by the government itself. This is usually followed by non-leftists posting pictures of publicly funded road crews, wherein four dudes will be standing around watching fifth man slowly shovel tar into a pothole. Thus is the efficiency of the glorious state.

JOKE #99: "Comrade"

A common greeting used by communists and socialists who will then totally deny having a hard-on for Stalinism or the USSR.

JOKE #100: "Smash the System"

A common chant leftists will repeat endlessly while throwing bottles at people and burning small businesses. Of course, they only want to smash the system long enough to appropriate more wealth for themselves, each one of them imagining that in the new system, they will be a significant person and not dead, enslaved, or in crushing poverty like has happened to most people after every prior leftist revolution.

JOKE #101: CHUD

Acronym for "Cannibalistic humanoid underground dwellers" taken from a cheesy 1984 film of the same name. Leftists briefly tried to use it to insult anyone who disagreed with them, spawning a million memes mocking their feeble attempt. Now it is used by some right wingers to describe themselves since the concept of juxtaposing the "Chud" with a soy sucking and weak wristed leftoid seemed too funny to not do.

THE END

www.ingramcontent.com/pod-product-compliance
Lightning Source LLC
Chambersburg PA
CBHW071505150726
48000CB00006B/2698